RED TED Art

RED TED Art

Cute and Easy Crafts for Kids

Maggy Woodley

■ SQUARE PEG

Published by Square Peg 2013

10 9 8 7 6 5 4 3 2 1

First published in Great Britain in 2013 by
Square Peg
Random House, 20 Vauxhall Bridge Road,
London SW1V 2SA
www.vintage-books.co.uk

Addresses for companies within The Random House Group Limited can be found at:
www.randomhouse.co.uk/offices.htm
The Random House Group Limited Reg. No. 954009

A CIP catalogue record for this book is available from the British Library

ISBN 9780224095556

The Random House Group Limited supports The Forest Stewardship Council (FSC®),
the leading international forest certification organisation. Our books carrying the FSC label
are printed on FSC® certified paper. FSC is the only forest certification scheme endorsed by
the leading environmental organisations, including Greenpeace. Our paper procurement
policy can be found at www.randomhouse.co.uk/environment

Typeset and designed by Anna Crone at www.siulendesign.com

Printed and bound in Germany by Firmengruppe APPL, aprinta druck, Wemding

To Max & Pippa
for continuingly
surprising me with
their creativity
and enthusiasm!

Contents

Introduction

I have always been incredibly passionate about making stuff, ever since I was a child. So, needless to say, I am a little biased and LOVE everything about crafting!

When I was little, I was lucky enough to have key individuals in my life – my adoptive grandmother Celia, in particular – who took the time to sit down with me to 'get crafty'. Celia was a wonderful influence in my life and taught me how to knit, to use the sewing machine, how to do cross stitch and generally encouraged my creativity. I remember making butterfly fairy cakes and sewing dolls and getting my Girl Guides craft badge. All this awakened and nurtured my love for making things and I often wonder whether I would be as creative now, without their influence. I will never know, but I have very fond memories of the times we had together and thank them dearly for it.

Now, as a mother, I enjoy taking the time to sit down with my two children and

make things with them. More than anything, I would love for them to look back on their childhood and remember the times we spent crafting together as special and magical. I love watching their little faces, brows furrowed with concentration as they cut, paint, glue and create – as well as their delight at playing with the finished product. They regularly impress and astound me with their ability and creative ideas.

We often get inspiration from our favourite books and songs – it's a great way to bring these to life as well as giving a focus to our crafts. Stuck for an idea? Turn to a book or a character, and ask yourself, how could we make that?

For these reasons, I love to encourage others to 'have a go'. Explore and have fun with your children and maybe discover an unknown passion for crafting. That is how my blog www.redtedart.com came into being when my son, then 2 years old,

was just old enough to start getting creative. We started with simple projects like scribbling on stars I had cut out for him or painting loo rolls that I would then put together into a small toy for him. He was enchanted and so was I. The blog was there to give me a 'regular focus' (it is so easy to say 'yes I will do it' and then never get round to it). Readers started coming and the blog began to grow. And as my readers grew, so did my son and our creativity. I started revisiting traditional crafts from my childhood, as well as inventing our own. And now we bring these together in this book.

Remember:

• Crafts do not have to be perfect (often the more imperfect the better!)

• Crafting does not always have to be messy (if that is something you are worried about). On the other hand, giving in to a little mess every now and then can be great fun!

It is all about having a go and trying out something new; making things YOUR way while at the same time spending time together and having fun.

This book is packed with craft ideas for all levels and age groups, ranging from the really simple to the slightly more challenging, and covering a range of techniques, from printing, painting and sewing, to some delicious edible crafts. Each project has step-by-step instructions and a list of the materials you will need, but you can also improvise with whatever materials you have to hand. Take the ideas as inspiration and make them your own.

Crafting doesn't have to cost the earth. Most of the ideas in this book use recycled materials from around the home, or items found on nature-walks, such as pine cones, twigs, stones and shells. That said, there are a few basics that are worth buying and having on hand.

Our basic craft box contains:

Paint

Poster paints come in a wide range of colours and are non-toxic and washable. Acrylic paints are useful when you need to create a durable surface. Always have plenty of paintbrushes to hand but there is no need to spend a lot of money on them.

Glue

Many of the projects in this book use PVA glue, which will stick lots of different materials. It is non-toxic and easy to use and dries clear. Buy good-quality PVA glue for the best results. Occasionally wood glue or a hot glue gun makes life easier. Glue sticks are useful for sticking paper and card together but are not as good for fiddly items. Masking tape and sticky tape are also useful to have to hand.

Googly eyes

These are indispensable! It is amazing how a simple twig or stone can be transformed with a pair of googly eyes.

Find self-adhesive ones or stick them on with PVA glue.

Scissors

Safety scissors are great when it comes to little hands. Have at least a couple of pairs of scissors: one for cutting paper and one for fabric. Pinking shears have a jagged edge and are great for cutting fabric to stop it fraying.

Basic sewing kit

Needles and cotton thread in several different colours are essential for sewing projects. An embroidery needle as well as a knitting needle (for making holes) is also useful.

Keep an eye out for things that can be put to good use. Over time we have gradually added other crafty items, some recycled, some bought. These include:

- Scraps of felt, fabric or funky foam
- Pipe cleaners
- Toilet rolls
- Ribbons and buttons (saved from gift packages or old clothes)
- Tissue paper and bubble wrap (also recycled from gifts)
- Coloured card

Occasionally, I can't resist 'specialist' craft items such as polymer clay. The important thing is to keep your eyes open and look for the crafting potential in everything!

11

Nuts

Racing walnut mice

Walnuts are a wonderful traditional item to craft with. The trick is to be able to split them into two perfect halves.

You will need:
Walnuts
Scraps of felt
Black marker pen or felt-tip pen
Marbles (one for each mouse)
Scissors
PVA glue

1 The older your walnut, the easier it will be to split it perfectly in half. Insert a knife or a pair of scissors into the round end of the walnut – this is its weakest point. Then tap, tap, tap the nut gently on a chopping board. Remove the nut from the inside. *With smaller children, and as ever when using knives or scissors, it's best for an adult to be on hand for this bit.*

2 Cut little ears and a strip for the tail from the felt in your chosen colours. You could also use string or a piece of ribbon as a tail.

3 Glue a pair of ears and a tail on to each walnut shell – tuck the end of the tail under the shell for a neater finish.

4 Add eyes, nose and whiskers with a pen.

5 Place a marble under each mouse and then let the mice race down a sloping book.

Which mouse will win?

Walnut boats

Walnut boats are super-quick and easy to make and great fun to play with.

You will need:
Walnuts
Toothpicks or small sticks
Scraps of paper or fabric or very wide colourful sticky tape (Washi tape)
Piece of old candle, Blu-tack or play dough
Scissors
PVA glue

Find a little puddle, birdbath or tub of water and let your boats sail!

1 Halve your walnuts (see Racing walnut mice, opposite.)

2 Prepare your masts. Snap the pointed top and bottom ends off each toothpick to make them a little shorter. Cut out some sails using coloured paper or fabric and glue them on to your toothpicks. Alternatively, use some wide colourful tape and double it over the toothpick. The benefit of using tape is that it can get wet without your sails getting soggy.

3 Light your candle and drip the wax into your walnut. *It's best to keep an eye on smaller children when using matches and candles.*

15

4 As the wax cools and becomes more solid, stick the mast in to it. Leave the wax to set firmly before launching your walnut boats. As an alternative to wax, use play dough or Blu-tack to secure your mast.

Peanut finger puppets

Have you ever looked at a peanut shell a little more closely? Have you turned it round in your hand and looked at its potential? If not, it is about time you did! Discovering shapes, animals and people in places you would least expect them can be great fun. Take a handful of humble peanuts and suddenly you have dwarves, witches and knights. Can you see them?

You will need:
Whole peanuts (in their shells)
Sharp serrated knife
Paints and paintbrushes
Fine black pen
Cotton wool
Scraps of felt, card and paper
Scissors
PVA glue

Snow White, the Seven Dwarves and the Wicked Witch

1 Use your knife to carefully 'saw' off the bottom end of your nine peanut shells – approximately one third from the end. *With smaller children, it's best for an adult to help with this bit.*

2 Wiggle out the nuts. It isn't the end of the world if you can't get both nuts out but they make a nice little snack whilst you are crafting! Set aside the longest peanut shell for Snow White and the most 'hunchbacked' shell for the Wicked Witch.

3 Paint coats and hats in your chosen colours on to the shells for the seven dwarves. For the Wicked Witch, paint the whole nut black, leaving a circular area free for the face. For Snow White, paint a bodice and skirt in your chosen colours, and then paint on some black hair. Leave to dry.

4 Once the paint has dried, add the final details such as eyes, nose and mouth, using a fine black pen.

5 To finish, glue a little cotton wool beard on to each dwarf and add a felt bow to Snow White's hair.

Knights

1 Follow Step 1 opposite and remove the nuts from the shells.

2 For each knight, paint the whole peanut shell in silver or grey paint, leaving a circular area free of paint for the face.

3 Once the paint has dried, add eyes and a mouth using a fine black pen.

4 Cut out a tiny shield from grey card and then another smaller shield from red or blue paper. Glue the red or blue paper on to the grey card and add details such as a cross or diagonal line with a black pen.

17

5 Glue a shield on to each knight, just below the face.

I think the knights would be fun in a home-made game of Noughts and Crosses!

Gumnut pencil toppers

Gumnuts are the hard fruits found on eucalyptus trees, and these gumnut pencil toppers are another example of 'spotting a shape' in everyday objects — notice how they have a perfect octopus head shape. If you can't find gumnuts near you, have a little hunt around and see what other things you might use instead, or mould the head shapes using air drying clay.

You will need:
Gumnuts
Paints and paintbrushes
Googly eyes
Pipe cleaners
Scissors
PVA glue

1 Paint your gumnut in your chosen colour.

2 Take two pipe cleaners and cut each one in half. Bend the four pieces over the end of a pencil — this will give you eight 'tentacles'.

3 Put a generous blob of glue inside the gumnut and insert the pencil with the pipe cleaners into the gumnut. Give it a good wiggle, arrange the legs a little and leave to dry.

4 Glue on a pair of googly eyes to bring your octopus to life.

Now get arty! What will you
draw with these octopencils?
Perhaps a seaside scene or a
ship with sunken treasure!

Walnut babies

These walnut babies make for adorable Christmas tree decorations, or additions to a doll's house. They make great little keepsakes too. Use old clothes or scraps of pretty patterned fabric for the tiny pillows and blankets.

You will need:
Walnuts
Narrow ribbon
Pipe cleaners
Wooden beads, approximately
  1.5 cm in diameter
Scraps of fabric
Fine black pen
Scissors
PVA glue

1 Halve your walnuts (see Racing walnut mice, page 14).

2 If you want to hang your walnut babies as tree decorations, take a piece of ribbon and glue each end in place on either side of the shell.

3 Coil a pipe cleaner around your finger to make a 'spring'. This will give the baby a body and help prop it up in its little bed. Glue a wooden bead on to one end of the pipe cleaner.

4 Cut a pillow from fabric and glue in place.

5 Stick the baby in place with a blob of glue and then glue on a little fabric scrap for a blanket. You will need to stick down the edges to avoid fraying.

6 Finally, use a pen to add the baby's eyes – make them wide-awake or sleeping – and a mouth.

Recycled Crafts

Toilet rolls

The cardboard tubes from toilet rolls and kitchen paper rolls are a free and surprisingly versatile craft material. You will be amazed by how many different things you can make with them, from fun craft projects to great home-made toys – there are literally hours of fun to be had.

Animal zoo

This animal zoo is easy to make and fun to play with. All you are doing is painting a toilet roll and then decorating it – so no fiddly legs to attach, no animals falling over and no arms coming loose. Simple fun that is simply fun!

You will need:
Toilet roll tubes
Paints and paintbrushes
Scraps of felt
Googly eyes (optional)
Fine black pen or felt-tip pens
Scissors
PVA glue

1 Decide which animals you would like to make. Paint your toilet roll in your chosen animal's colour, such as yellow for a lion or grey for an elephant. However, you don't have to stick to traditional colours – why not go bright and colourful instead?

2 Once the paint is dry, use a pair of scissors to cut out any details such as ears and feet by snipping away the bits you don't need.

3 Decide what extra features your animal needs, such as a mane for a lion, tusks for an elephant or spots for a giraffe, and cut these from scraps of felt. Glue these in place and add googly eyes (if using). You can, of course, paint the features on too.

4 Add any extra details for the face with a pen.

Superheroes

If you don't fancy making animals, then how about creating people out of your toilet rolls. You can make a family, pirates, princesses – whatever takes your fancy! Here we have superheroes. Before you start, think about how you want your superhero to look. Superheroes tend to wear bright colours, often with an emblem across their chest. They can wear masks, belts, pants and capes – it's up to you!

You will need:
Toilet roll or kitchen roll tubes
Skin-coloured paint and paintbrush
Scraps of felt and fabric in bright
  colours
Googly eyes
Fine black pen
Scissors
PVA glue

Now put on your best superhero voice and go and rescue some toilet roll animals from disaster!

1 Paint the top third of your paper roll in your desired skin colour (this will become the head of your superhero).

2 Look at the fabrics and felt pieces you have and decide what kind of superhero you could make. Cut out the basic body suit and glue in place and add your googly eyes.

3 Cut capes, masks and emblems in the coloured felt that you want to use. Alternatively you can make a mask by gluing on a piece of ribbon with holes cut out for the eyes. Glue in place and add any other details such as belts, buttons or buckles.

4 Finally, use a pen to give your superhero a brave and fearless face and to add any other fine details you wish.

Monsters

Monsters are always great fun to make. You can make them in any colour and add all sorts of embellishments – a perfect craft for using up the odds and ends in your craft drawer. As monsters are an odd bunch, you can do what you like: one eye, five eyes, spots or stripes, hair or fur... your choice is limitless!

You will need:
Toilet roll tubes
Paints and paintbrushes
Googly eyes
Scraps of fabric, tissue paper,
* card and funky foam*
Pipe cleaners (optional)
PVA glue

1 Paint your monsters the desired base colour.

2 Press down the front and back of the top of your toilet roll to create a little dip and two pointy ears.

3 Glue on the googly eyes, and use your bits and pieces of craft material to add stripes, spots, hair – whatever takes your fancy. You could also make a small hole on either side and thread a pipe cleaner through to make arms.

Marionettes

Toilet rolls also make great marionettes. Use one roll for the body and another for the head and then connect with strings and paper. We made a sausage dog and some giraffes overleaf... but what could you come up with?

Sausage dog

You will need:
1 kitchen roll tube
1 toilet roll tube
Paints and paintbrushes
Conkers (in season) or bottle lids
Googly eyes
String
Skewer or knitting needle
* for piercing holes*
Small twig
Sticks or wooden skewer
Large-eyed needle
Scissors
PVA glue

1. Paint the cardboard tubes all over in your chosen colour. Paint as much of the inside as you can, as you will be able to see inside the tubes. Leave to dry.

2. Shape the dog's head by cutting five equally spaced slits in the toilet roll, about 3 cm long. Squeeze the sides together by pressing on the ends of the roll so that each of the sides overlaps: this forms a pointy nose for the dog. Add glue and hold in place with an elastic band or piece of string. Make sure you do not accidentally glue the band on.

3. Cut a little off one end of the kitchen towel roll and use the trimming to cut ear shapes. Glue these on to the dog's head. Glue on the googly eyes.

4. Now make the feet and tail. Start by piercing a hole through each conker using a skewer or knitting needle – if you can't get hold of conkers you can use plastic bottle lids. *An adult should help with this bit.* Then make holes in the long roll: one for the tail and four for the feet (see diagram on p154). Cut a piece of string about 10 cm long and tie a knot at one end. Use a large-eyed needle to thread a conker on to the string and then feed the needle through one front arm hole and out the other front arm hole. Thread on another conker and secure with a knot: these will be the dog's front legs. Repeat to make the back legs. For the tail, stick the twig through the hole and secure with lots of glue.

5. Now take the dog's head and pierce it twice – once at the top (roughly between the ears) and once below. Pierce a hole at the front end of the long body roll. Tie a knot at the end of a piece of string and thread it through the hole in the body and both holes in the head – the end of the string will be one of your 'handles'. Make another hole in the dog's body, near the tail. Tie a knot at the end of another piece of string and thread this through the body – this will be the other 'handle'.

6. Tie both pieces of string to each end of a stick or wooden skewer to complete your marionette.

Giraffe

You will need:
2 toilet roll tubes
Paints and paintbrushes
Sheets of coloured paper
  in two colours
Googly eyes
String
Sticks or wooden skewers
Scissors
PVA glue, glue stick

1 Cut one of the toilet rolls in half to make the head. Paint the body and head in your chosen colours.

2 Make five paper 'ladders' for the giraffe's legs and neck. Cut two sheets of different coloured A4 paper lengthwise into strips, 1–2 cm wide. Take a strip of each colour (colour A and colour B). Glue strip A on to strip B at a right angle. Fold strip B over A, then fold A over B, and so on, to the end of your strip. If your ladder needs to be longer, use a glue stick to attach a second strip. Continue until your ladders are the desired length. Cut off any excess paper and glue down the edges to finish.

Method continued overleaf…

3 Cut some more strips of paper, this time into 5 mm-wide strips. Make two smaller ladders — these will be the giraffe's horns.

4 Cut small triangles of paper for the ears. Glue the eyes, ears and horns on to the smaller paper roll to make the giraffe's head.

5 Attach one end of the neck ladder to the head and the other end to the body with glue. Attach the four legs to the body.

6 Take the two sticks or skewers and cross them to make a handle for your marionette. Tie them together with string.

7 To assemble the marionette, use a knife or skewer to make two holes at the front and back of the giraffe (see diagram on p154), and one on the top of the giraffe's head. Thread a long piece of string through the holes in the body and tie the ends to one of your sticks. Tie a knot in a second, shorter piece of string. Starting inside the toilet roll, thread through the hole in the giraffe's head and tie to your second stick.

Blossom fairy lights

Love fairy lights? Why not make some of your own? Decorate a plain set of lights with your very own egg box flowers and blossoms.

You will need:
Egg boxes
Paints and paintbrushes
Pink, gold and blue glitter
Nail scissors
Plain fairy lights
Scissors
PVA glue

1. Cut your egg box into individual cups. You can either leave the cups plain or cut out little petal shapes with small scissors.

2. Paint the cups both inside and out – we used pink for blossoms and yellow for daffodils. Allow to dry.

3. Paint some PVA glue on the inside of your flowers, but not the centre as you will be cutting a hole here later. Tip a small amount of glitter into the cup and shake it so that the glitter sticks. Pour glitter into the next cup and repeat until all the cups are 'glittered'. Allow to dry completely.

4. Using nail scissors, cut small slits across the top centre of each. Gently push a fairy light right through each flower cup making sure the bulb isn't touching the cardboard.
Always switch off fairy lights if you are leaving the room.

Clothes peg people

There is something irresistible about clothes peg people. Is it that you can turn a clothes peg into virtually any character you want? Or is it that you can take them with you wherever you go? Whatever it is, clothes peg people are a must! Here we've made a ballerina, a royal guard, a mermaid and a superhero.

You will need:
Traditional wooden clothes pegs
Acrylic paints and paintbrushes
Scraps of fabric, ribbon and felt
Felt-tip pens
PVA glue

1 Paint your clothes peg in your character's basic colours. For example, the ballerina has black hair, a pink bodice and black shoes; the soldier has a red tunic, black trousers and gold buttons; the pirate has a stripy shirt and blue trousers; the superhero has a yellow suit, green pants and red boots.

2 When they are dry, add the fabric details. To make a tutu for the ballerina, use a needle and thread to stitch a line of running stitch around a scrap of pink tulle (see p159 for diagrams for different stitches). Pull the threads to gather the tulle around the ballerina's body. Hide the edges by gluing on a strip of narrow ribbon.

3 Make the soldier's bearskin by cutting a piece of black felt into a rectangle. Glue to the soldier's head in a cylinder shape. Press and glue the top together and then cut round the top of the bearskin in a semicircle shape.

4 For the superhero, cut a cape from a scrap of fabric and glue around the neck. Add more glue to a small piece of ribbon and secure in place around the superhero's neck.

5 For the mermaid, paint the body, add glitter sprinkles or sequins. To make her fish tail, cut a semicircle out of card, paint it blue or green. For hair, take 12 strands of 9 cm long wool, tie a knot around the wool on either side to create nice bunches, and glue on to the head (see diagram on p154).

6 Use felt-tip pens to add eyes and a mouth, as well as any other details.

Note: Adding the fabric pieces can be a little fiddly. Be patient, work slowly and you will manage it. Sometimes, it helps to hold things in place with an elastic band while they dry.

Gloves & Socks

Monkey

Most people have at least one odd sock and one odd glove floating around their home. Or maybe your glove has a hole in it? What to do with them? Make little plush toys, of course!

Cuddly toys are much loved in our house. They are invited to tea parties. They join us on trips in the car and they look after us when we sleep. They also make great gifts for friends.

This little monkey can be made out of either a pair of old children's tights or a pair of socks. Tights are a little easier, as you have more leeway when cutting. You will need two socks or legs as one will be for the body of the monkey and the other will make up the arm, tail, ears and mouth.

You will need:
Pair of children's socks or
* tights cut to make two socks of the*
* desired length*
Needle and sewing thread
Stuffing
Buttons or scraps of felt
Embroidery thread
Scissors

1 Take your first sock. The heel of the sock will be the monkey's bottom and the toe its face. Cut in a straight line from the top edge at the back of the sock all the way to the top of the heel. Make a parallel cut at the front. This creates the monkey's two legs (see diagrams on p155). Turn each flap inside out and fold each leg over lengthways so that the right sides are facing. Stitch along the seams, leaving an opening near the heel. Turn right way out, stuff both legs and the body and head of the monkey, and stitch the opening near the heel closed.

2 Take your second sock. Use the diagram on p155 to show you where to cut out two arms, a tail, the mouth and ears.

3 Take an arm piece and fold in half lengthways, right sides together. Stitch along the seams, keeping the top open, then turn right side out and stuff. Repeat for second arm. Stitch both arms to the monkey's body, tucking in the raw edges as you go along to create a neat seam.

4 Repeat step three to make the tail.

5 Cut out the heel of the second sock for the mouth. Position the mouth on the front of the monkey's face with a little stuffing underneath. Tuck the raw edges under and pin in place. Stitch neatly to join the mouth securely to the face.

6 Take the four pieces of fabric for the ears. Place two pieces right sides together and stitch round the seams, leaving the bottom of the ear open. Repeat for the second ear. Turn right way out and tuck in the edges. Pinch the centre of the ear to give it some shape and sew on to the monkey.

7 For the eyes you can either sew on some buttons or glue on some felt circles. Finally, stitch a mouth for your monkey, using embroidery thread.

41

The owl and the pussy-cat

Making toys out of gloves is a great craft for the beginner sewer. Usually there is no cutting of the glove involved, which means no fraying if things are not sewn as neatly as they could be. Also, you can usually choose to glue on some of the details, making the sewing bit of the craft a little bit easier. Try making this cute owl and pussy-cat from the famous poem by Edward Lear.

You will need:
Old gloves (one per toy)
Buttons
Scraps of felt
Stuffing
Needle and thread
Ribbon (for cat)
Scissors
PVA glue (optional)

1 Both the owl and the pussy-cat start off in the same way. Turn your glove inside out and lay flat. Sew across the fingers and thumb (see diagram on p156) so that the little and index fingers become the ears.

2 Turn your glove back the right way round and ease out the ears. This may take a little fiddling.

3 Stuff your glove. You can shape your toy whilst you are stuffing and neaten out any unevenness.

4 For the owl: depending on the size of your glove, you may have to tuck in a little of the wrist cuff before you stitch it shut. Before doing so, cut some owl feet from your felt, and sew these into your seam as you go along.

5 For the cat: don't tuck the wrist cuff in, just sew it shut (your cat will be taller than the owl). Shape the head by stitching a line of running stitch (see diagram on p159) just below where you want your cat's head to be. Pull the threads tight to gather the fabric and shape the head. For a simpler alternative, use an elastic band, and then hide the elastic with the cat's ribbon.

6 Now make your owl an owl by adding big bright eyes, a beak and some wings. You can either stitch the buttons and beak on, as shown here, or use PVA glue. If gluing, use circles of felt for the eyes instead of buttons. (Some cheaper types of synthetic felt may not glue well, in which case you should sew on the features.) Here they are all sewn on (securing the eyes with the buttons, the beak with stitches across the top and the wings with a short running stitch). Sew or glue a tummy and felt eyes and a nose to the cat's face, add a pretty ribbon around its neck and you're done!

43

Octopus

This octopus is another great craft for beginner sewers. There is only a little sewing needed (to secure the head in place) and the rest is stuffing and a little cutting. Smaller children's tights are best, ideally for ages one to two, otherwise you will end up with a giant octopus! There is only one clever bit for this octopus – get it right and it will be finished in no time. You know when you put two socks together and turn the top over to make a pair? This is the principal applied to the octopus. However, when you turn your sock like this, the top of the sock is always inside out, whilst the toes of the sock are the right way. Follow these instructions to make sure your octopus looks right.

You will need:
4 pairs woollen tights, preferably
* for ages 1–2*
Toy stuffing
Needle and thread
Scraps of felt
Scissors
PVA glue

1 Stuff all eight legs of your tights from the toe to about halfway up the leg.

2 Create your head by taking the pair of tights that will become the head (in this case the blue tights) and cutting a hole in the gusset. (See p156 for diagrams.) Lay this pair of tights in front of you with the stuffed legs pointing towards you. Take the legs and push them up through the hole in the gusset. You should now have the legs pointing up through the top part of the tights as in the picture opposite.

3 Stuff the head with the unstuffed tops of the remaining three pairs of tights and arrange the legs so that they all alternate in colour.

4 Add some toy stuffing to fill out and shape the head, then stitch all around the hem of the first pair of tights to secure the head and all the legs in place.

5 Cut eyes from scraps of felt and glue or stitch in place.

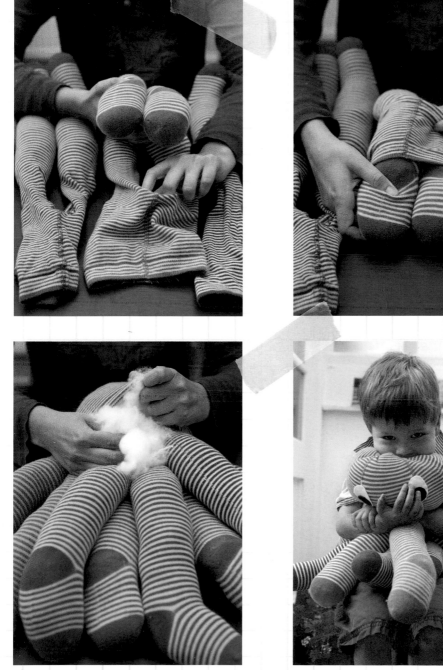

Hobby horse

Another craft for lone socks – a larger sock is best for this, so hunt out one of Dad's stray ones! You can also use a child's sock to make some fun mini horses.

You will need:
Sock
Sturdy stick or broom handle
  (the stick should be the height
  of the child or slightly longer)
Saw
Stuffing
Scraps of fabric or felt
Sticky tape
String
Ball of wool
Buttons
Ribbon
Needle and thread
Scissors

1 Prepare your stick by sawing off any branches or twigs. Add a notch about 20–30 cm down from the top – this will help hold the head in place. *An adult should help with this step.*

2 Cover the top of the stick with stuffing or bubble wrap and some fabric scraps and tape in place – this will protect the horse's head later and prevent the stick from poking out.

3 Start stuffing your sock from the toe up to the heel. You should be able to shape the head with your hands to form a muzzle and head. Insert the stick and then add stuffing all around it, reshaping the head if necessary.

4 Wrap a piece of string tightly around the base of the head and stick, and tie tightly to fix the stick to the head at the same height as the notch you cut earlier.

5 Cut out two tear-shaped pieces of felt for the ears, and then another two smaller pieces of felt for the insides of the ears. It is nice to have two contrasting colours. Stitch or glue them together and pinch at the bottom to create an ear shape. Pin them in the right position (they will be secured later). You could also use denim for the ears as for the horse here, but it requires a little more sewing to avoid fraying edges.

6 Pin the buttons for the eyes where you think you will want them – you may want to reposition them later.

7 Cut your ribbon into several lengths to create the halter. You need a piece to go around the muzzle, a piece to go around the head and a much longer piece that connects the muzzle with the headpiece and then forms the reins. It should loop back around the head and connect on the other side with the headpiece and nozzle.

8 Pin the ribbon pieces on to the head to see if you have them in the right place. Check that the eyes, ears and halter all work nicely together and then sew everything in place.

9 Make the mane and forelock by marking a line from the top of the head between the ears to where you want the mane to end. Cut several lengths of wool to 20 cm. Form a loop with each length of wool and stitch it to the back of the horse's head with a firm stitch. Repeat with the remaining lengths of wool all the way down the back of the head to form the mane. Repeat on the top of the head at the front to make the forelock.

Giddy-up! And off you gallop.

Printing

Apple prints

It is great fun to explore what kind of printed shapes 'things' make. A popular print is the humble apple. Cut it one way and you get an apple shape; cut it another and you get a wonderful little star shape. As apple prints are quite big, they are great for decorating things quickly and so are ideal for making your own wrapping paper. Here are two ideas for printing with apples. But why stop at just these two? Use fabric paint to add apple shapes to T-shirts or canvas bags. Or keep it super simple and make greetings cards or party invites with them.

Wrapping paper

You will need:
Roll of white paper, brown packing
  paper or sheets of newspaper
1–2 apples
Red and green paint
Dish for paint
Knife

1 Decide on what pattern you would like to make. For the classic apple shape, cut your apple from top to bottom through the middle. For a star shape, cut the apple across horizontally.

2 Put your paint on to plates. Dip the apple half in the paint then press it lightly on to some scrap paper to remove any excess paint. There is a technique to getting it right. Don't add too much paint or it will squirt out of the sides and you won't have a neat edge. Often the second or third print is better than the first.

3 Prepare your paper and get printing. As apple prints are so vibrant they will look great on all sorts of paper – including newspaper – making for fun, alternative and thrifty wrapping paper.

Halloween goodie bags

Have you ever noticed that the apple shape also looks just like a jack-o'-lantern? Use these bags to go trick or treating, or fill with goodies at a Halloween party!

You will need:
Paper bags
Apple
Orange paint
Dish for paint
Black paint or black pen
Knife

1 Cut your apple vertically to give you the classic apple shape and remove the stalk.

2 Put some orange paint on to a plate and dip the apple half into it. Press it lightly on to some scrap paper to remove any excess paint. Print all over the bags and leave to dry.

3 Add jack-o'-lantern details, either with black paint or a black pen.

51

Potato print cityscape

Potato printing is one of those hugely versatile crafts – there are so many different patterns and shapes you can cut into a potato that the possibilities are endless. You can make greetings cards and wrapping paper or printed artwork to suit different occasions or seasons. Either cut a pattern into the potato yourself or use a cookie cutter to help guide your shape. Follow these instructions to make cityscape cards.

You will need:
2–3 potatoes of medium size
Knife
White card cut down to postcard size (one sheet of A4 will give you 4 postcards)
Poster paint
Dish for paint

1 Cut your potato in half and then slice round the edges to make a rectangle shape. Add little squares for windows and use the tip of your knife to remove the centres. Create a few more in different sizes. *With smaller children, an adult should help with the cutting.* The smallest size can be used to build up a long, thin skyscraper shape. It can also double as a bus if used horizontally.

2 Dry the potato with a paper towel and pour some paints on to a paint dish. Dip the potato in the paint and practise making your prints on some scrap paper.

3 Print your cards. Make 3–4 skyscraper prints, some other buildings and houses and the odd bus, using different coloured paints. You'll need to wash and dry the potato for each colour change. Then use your fingers to finger-paint some trees and clouds and some wheels for the bus. With a pen, add any details such a tree trunk or little birds in the sky.

Foot and hand print fish

This foot and hand print collage is a great project to do as a family or with a small group of friends. It can get a little messy but that's all part of the fun!

You will need:
Finger paints
Paper
Felt-tip pens
Roll of coloured paper
 (for background)
Scissors
PVA glue

1 Create a number of hand and foot prints by painting hands and feet in a variety of colours and pressing them gently on to sheets of paper. Get friends and family members to join in so you can create different sized fish.

2 Select your favourite prints and, with a pen, add fish outlines, including eyes, mouths and fins. Make them all different and then cut them out.

3 Glue your fish on to the coloured background paper.

Stand back and admire!

Fingerprint cards

Fingerprint cards are super quick and easy to make and look adorable. They make great birthday cards for relatives, as well as Easter cards or 'thank you' cards.

You will need:
Card stock (you can fold your own
*   cards or buy ready-made blanks)*
White paper
Finger paint
Fine black marker pen
Scissors, pinking shears or a ruler
Glue stick

1 Decide on your design. We made bees, ladybirds, chicks (great for Easter) and flowers. Hearts are nice, too, for Mother's Day or Valentine's cards.

2 Make your prints by dipping your finger into the paint, and then pressing it on to the paper. Practise on some scrap paper and make a few extra prints, in case you smudge some of them. For a heart, make two fingerprints angled on top of each other. For the other designs, you can either do individual prints or sets of two or three.

3 Once your fingerprints have dried, use a fine black marker to add embellishments such as eyes, beaks and wings.

4 Cut around your designs with scissors or pinking shears. Alternatively you can tear along the edge of a ruler for a rougher look. Create squares or rectangles highlighting each design.

5 Glue on to your card stock.

Write a lovely message, pop in the post and make someone smile!

Bubble wrap trees

Bubble wrap is great for printing. You can use it for many things, including this 'four seasons' picture. This is a piece of art which can be created by even very young crafters – here a three-year-old was at work!

You can either revisit this activity every season and do one painting at a time, or all in one go on one large sheet of paper.

You will need:
Card or cardboard
Sheet of white paper
Bubble wrap
Paints and paintbrushes
Black pen
Scissors
PVA glue

1 Think about what you want to include in your picture for each season. For example you might want to change the colours of the sky and ground. For spring we made bubble wrap blossom for the trees and fingerprint lambs; summer has sunflowers and butterflies, autumn has leaves on the ground and hedgehogs and winter has snow and robins.

2 Mark your sheet of paper into four areas and paint your background in the relevant colours.

3 Cut tree shapes from your card or cardboard and paint them dark brown. Glue the trees on to the background.

4 Cut your bubble wrap to the size of your tree. Using a brush, paint the bubble side in your chosen colour, for example, pink for spring blossom, green for summer leaves, brown for autumn leaves and white for winter snow. Print on to your paper.

5 Make fingerprints for the sheep, hedgehogs and robins. Add any extra details to your fingerprints with black pen.

Stones

Stone family

Stones come in all sorts of shapes and sizes. This craft is for those perfectly flat stones that are used for skimming. For each member of the family you'll need one smaller flat stone for the head and one bigger stone for the body. It is best to use acrylic paint as the stones will last longer. Acrylic paint also allows you to add layer over layer, such as white on top of black.

You will need:
Selection of flat stones in various
  sizes
Acrylic paints and paintbrushes
Black marker pen

1 Sort your stones into possible 'people' combinations. A small round or triangular stone might make a good head, and try different combinations of long thin bodies, or squat round ones.

2 Decide what kind of stone people you'd like to create: here we have a traditional family – a father in a suit, a mother in a dress, a boy in a stripy top and a girl in a pink dress. But you could also make them a bit eccentric – what about a family of aliens or vampires?

3 Paint your stones in layers, leaving each layer to dry completely before adding the next colour or detail. Begin with flesh colour for the heads and the base colour for the clothes. Then add the next layer – for example, paint hair on to the heads and arm shapes on to the bodies. If you make a mistake, don't worry, just paint over and start again.

4 If you are painting someone you know, add little personal details, such as a child's favourite toy bunny or Dad's favourite colour tie!

5 Add the eyes, nose and mouth with a marker pen.

Now you are ready to play or display. See what happens when you swap the people's heads around!

Five little ducks

And their mummy duck! These little stone ducks are great to play with. You can sing with them, count with them, make up stories with them, or decorate your desk with them. Wouldn't they look sweet on a little shelf in your bedroom? Acrylic paint is best for this project, as it won't rub off. However you can use ordinary poster paint and varnish it afterwards.

You will need:
6 stones
Yellow and white acrylic paints
Paintbrushes
Black and red or orange markers

1 Go on a stone hunt in your garden or local park and collect stones of all sizes. When you get home, wash and thoroughly dry them.

2 Sort through your stones. Which stones smile at you as potential little ducks? Can you make them stand upright? You'll need one large stone for the 'mummy' duck and five smaller ones, ranging from small to medium, for the little ducks.

3 Paint your large stone white and the five smaller ones yellow. Leave them to dry on a piece of cling film or greaseproof paper (they will stick to newspaper).

4 When they are completely dry, add details with marker pens – two black eyes and a little red or orange beak for each duck.

Five Little Ducks

FIVE little ducks went
 swimming one day
Over the hill and far away.
Mother duck said QUACK
 QUACK QUACK QUACK
And only **FOUR** little ducks
 came back!

FOUR little ducks went
 swimming one day
Over the hill and far away.
Mother duck said QUACK
 QUACK QUACK QUACK
And only **THREE** little ducks
 came back!

THREE little ducks went
 swimming one day
Over the hill and far away.
Mother duck said QUACK
 QUACK QUACK QUACK
And only **TWO** little ducks
 came back!

TWO little ducks went
 swimming one day
Over the hill and far away.
Mother duck said QUACK
 QUACK QUACK QUACK
And only **ONE** little duck
 came back!

ONE little duck went
 swimming one day
Over the hill and far away.
Mother duck said QUACK
 QUACK QUACK QUACK
And all her **FIVE** little ducks
 came back!

Crayon and rock paperweights

These paperweights are really quick and easy to make. They make lovely gifts for Father's Day or 'just because' and feel wonderfully tactile to hold. They are also a brilliant way to use up any crayon odds and ends you may have lying around.

You will need:
1 large smooth stone for each paperweight
Old wax crayons in assorted colours, paper removed
Oven gloves
Newspaper
Heatproof surface

1 Place the stones in the oven and bake for 15–20 minutes at 180°C/350°F. The stones need to be very hot.

2 Prepare your work surface. Place several layers of newspaper on top of a heatproof surface such as a wooden chopping board. You will find that the wax melts right through the paper, so make sure you use lots of layers, and don't use your best board!

3 With the oven gloves, remove one hot stone at a time from the oven and place it on your work surface. *An adult should supervise this bit – the stones will be very hot!*

4 Take a piece of crayon and gently rest it on your stone. Move it gently across the stone, letting the crayon wax melt and run down the sides. Repeat with the next colour and keep going until you are happy with the design. The colours will mix and mingle beautifully. We used rainbow colours: red, orange, yellow, light green, green, blue, purple and pink. Try creating a different effect by using the same colours but in reverse order.

5 Let the stones cool down completely. You will find a small pool of crayon will have collected at the bottom – you may wish to give this a good rub, so that it doesn't come off when the stone is used as a paperweight.

Sewing & Fabric Crafts

Nature bag

These quick and easy little bags are sewn from old jumpers that have shrunk and felted in the wash – yes, it happens! Use them as your 'nature' bag – perfect for taking on walks and bringing nature's treasures to craft with.

You will need:
Old felted jumper or large piece
 of felt
Scissors
Pins
Embroidery needle and thread
Button
Wool

1 Cut a rectangle of fabric from your felted jumper or felt piece that is approximately A4 size.

2 Fold the bottom third over to make the pocket and pin in place. Leave the top third free.

3 Using a contrasting embroidery thread and blanket stitch (see p159), sew along one side, starting at the folded corner. Continue along the top of the flap and carry on down the second side until you get to the other corner. You could also use running stitch (see p159) but blanket stitch gives a neater edge and looks smarter.

4 Make a buttonhole by cutting a hole in the centre of the flap. Sew blanket stitch around the edge of the hole. Fold the flap over and mark the position of the button, just behind the buttonhole. Sew in place.

5 Cut six 30 cm lengths of wool for the strap. Tie a knot at one end, leaving a couple of inches for a tassel, then plait the threads together, taking two strands at a time. Leave a little tassel at the other end and tie a knot to fasten it. Sew the ends of the strap to the two top corners of the bag.

Organza flowers

Who can resist a pretty flower? These make lovely hair accessories or brooches and make a great addition to a bag or backpack. They would also look gorgeous on a fairy or princess outfit. This is a great craft to enthuse older children to have a go.

You will need:
Synthetic fabric such as organza
  (which is a bit like very fine tulle)
Thin card
Needle and thread
Buttons
Candle and matches
Scissors

1 Draw three circles of decreasing size on a piece of thin card and cut them out. These will form your templates. The flowers made here were made with circles 4.5 cm, 5.5 cm and 6.5 cm in diameter.

2 Use your templates to cut out circles of organza – you will need two of each size (six per flower). Don't worry if your circles aren't perfect – organza is hard to cut and the next steps will help even out your petal shapes.

3 Take one circle at a time and make six even snips around the flower to make petal outlines.

4 Now comes the fun bit! Light your candle and carefully and gently melt the edges of each petal. Repeat with the other five circles. It is very easy to completely burn your organza, so take care. If you get slightly singed edges, you can trim these off with nail scissors and seal again. *An adult should supervise this step.*

5 Put the singed circles together with the largest at the bottom and the smallest at the top. Use a needle and thread to secure with a few small stitches in the centre and then sew a button.

Fabric mâché bowls

Fabric mâché works using the same technique as papier mâché – simply use strips of fabric scraps and PVA glue to create bowls – just as you would with newspaper. The bowls are pretty enough to give as gifts, and are fun to make too. Think about what pattern you want to create – maybe using one patterned fabric for the outside of your bowl and another for the inside.

You will need:
Bowl (to use as mould)
Cling film
Shallow dish for glue
*Strips and small scraps of fabric (old
  shirts or cotton dresses work well)*
Scissors
PVA glue

1 Choose a bowl to use as your mould. Cover the outside completely with a layer of cling film (this is to stop your work from sticking to the mould).

2 Put some PVA glue in a shallow bowl and water down so that it is roughly one part water and two parts glue.

3 Soak the fabric pieces in the diluted PVA mixture. Start to layer your mould with the soggy fabric, making sure that the pattern is face down. Cover the whole of the outside of the mould with one layer of fabric strips. This will become the inside of your bowl.

4 Add another layer to the outside, again with the pattern facing down.

5 Now add a third layer, but this time make sure the pattern faces up. This is the outer side of your bowl. Leave to dry overnight (or longer if necessary).

6 Once the bowl is completely dry you can ease it out of the mould. You may find that it is a little tricky so use the cling film to help guide the bowl off. Sometimes the cling film will stick to the fabric – you can either carefully peel it off or leave it as it is for a shiny finished look. Trim around the edges with a pair of scissors or leave rough for effect.

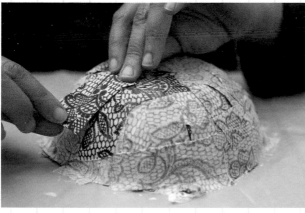

Juggling chooks

These juggling 'chooks' are simple little beanbags (actually they are filled with rice) which are a lot easier to make than they look. Once you have made one, you will want to make another and another and another. They make great little juggling sets as presents.

You will need:
20 x 11 cm patterned fabric (for each chook)
Scraps of felt
Rice
Toy stuffing
Needle and thread
Scissors

1 Lay your fabric out in front of you, right side up and short edge at the bottom. Cut a comb, beak and wattle from scraps of felt and position them at the top right-hand corner of the fabric, pointing in (see diagram on p156). Then fold your fabric up so that the right sides are together. Be sure not to have the felt comb too close to the right-hand edge, as you may sew it by accident.

2 Pin and stitch in place across the top and right-hand side, leaving a 1 cm seam allowance. Leave the left-hand side open for stuffing. Turn right side out. Work out where the eyes should go and then sew a French knot on either side (see p159).

3 Push a little stuffing into the head and then add some rice, about 50–60 g per chook.

4 To create the pyramid shape, take point A and point B (see diagram, p156) and bring them together in the centre. Point C and point D will become your new ends, giving you a pyramid. It sounds tricky, but try it and it will all make sense! Tuck in the edge of the fabric to create a neat seam and sew.

iPod case

Crafts that have a practical element always carry extra appeal for me. Why not take some old fabric scraps and make a cool case for your iPod or phone? This involves a little fabric placing 'magic' that seems tricky, but follow the steps and hey presto! It comes out perfectly.

You will need:
Fabric for the outside of the case
  (old jeans or similar fabric is perfect)
Microfibre or lining fabric
8 cm ribbon or elastic
Button
Needle and thread
Scissors

1 For the outer case, cut one 20 x 10 cm piece fabric for the back and one 14 x 10 cm piece for the front. For the lining, cut one 15 x 10 cm piece and one 14 x 10 cm piece. (See diagram on p157.)

2 Place the larger piece of lining fabric on top of the back case fabric, right sides together. Make a loop from the ribbon or elastic and position it between the two layers with the loop facing in. Pin the layers together. Starting 6.5 cm from the loop end, stitch up the side, along the top and 6.5 cm down the other side again, leaving a 5 mm seam allowance. This will become the flap of your wallet.

3 To make the front of your case, place the two smaller pieces of fabric right sides together. Sew across one top edge only. Flip the lining over, so that the right sides now face out.

4 Lift up the lower half of the lining on the larger piece of fabric. Lay the smaller piece on top of the larger piece. The right sides of the fabric (in this case denim) will be facing each other. The top of the smaller pieces should be aligned with the 6.5 cm flap you sewed earlier. If they don't align perfectly, you can trim a little of the bottom. Fold the flap you lifted back down.

5 Now sew all around the bottom of your case from the edge of the flap all the way round to the stitching on the other side, leaving a 5 mm seam allowance. You will have one remaining opening – use this to turn your cover right side out.

6 Turn down the flap and mark where the button should be. Sew on your button and you are done.

Magic!

Felt food

Felt food is a great addition to any play kitchen or teddy bear's picnic. Make your own doughnuts with different sprinkles. What would you put on yours? Or how about a bowl full of strawberries? Yummy.

Doughnuts

You will need:
Selection of felt sheets for the doughnuts and icing (cream, brown, blue and pink)
Beads or embroidery thread for sprinkles
Thin strips of felt
Toy stuffing
Needle and thread
Scissors

1 Cut two doughnut circles from brown or cream felt and one icing circle from blue felt. A CD makes a good template.

2 Now add the sprinkles detail to the icing. You can do this by stitching on beads or by using embroidery thread to make French knots (see page 159). Alternatively, cut thin strips of coloured felt and stitch to the icing using a running stitch (see page 159).

3 Sew the icing on to one of the doughnut circles.

4 Place the two doughnut pieces together, right sides facing. Pin in place and then stitch all round the outer edge, leaving a gap of about 3–4 cm for stuffing.

5 Turn right side out and then stitch around the edge of the central hole, keeping the stitches small.

6 Fill the doughnut with stuffing and sew the gap closed to finish.

Strawberries

You will need:
Sheet of red felt
Scraps of dark and light green felt
Needle and red sewing thread
Yellow embroidery thread
Toy stuffing

1 Cut out circles of red felt about 12 cm in diameter. Cut each circle in half. Each semicircle will make one strawberry.

2 Thread a needle with yellow embroidery thread and sew small running stitches to represent the seeds. Space them out evenly.

3 Fold the semicircle in half wrong side out and sew along the straight edge. Turn right side out.

4 With red thread, sew a line of running stitch 5 mm from the edge all around the circle edge. Gently pull the thread to gather the edge slightly. Add a little stuffing, pull the threads to close up. Sew in place.

5 Cut a flower shape from the dark green felt, and a smaller circle from the light green felt. Place the circle on top of the flower shape and sew both pieces to the top of the strawberry with a large cross stitch. Alternate the light green and dark green on the other strawberries for variety.

Modelling Crafts

Salt Dough

Salt dough is a wonderfully inexpensive and fun modelling material that you can easily make at home. It can be air-dried or dried in the oven, thus preserving your creations for ever. For this reason salt dough makes lovely keepsakes or gifts. Traditional salt dough crafts include Christmas tree decorations made using shaped cookie cutters. You can also try making salt dough beads and pendants.

Basic salt dough recipe

You will need:
2 cups of plain flour
1 cup of salt
1 cup of water (maximum)
Food colouring or paint to colour
  (optional)
Mixing bowl
Baking tray
Greaseproof paper
Oven gloves

Note: Different brands of paint have a different effect on the salt dough – some make it stickier than others (in which case, add more flour and salt). Other paints may fade when the salt dough dries. Experiment to see which paints work best for you. You can also try using food colouring or leave your salt dough plain, then paint your creations afterwards.

1 Put the flour and salt in a bowl and very gradually stir in the water – no more than half a cup to start with. Salt dough should not be sticky to handle; if it is, add more flour and salt to the bowl.

2 If you are adding colour to your dough, add it now and knead well. It will be quite messy at first, but the more you work the colour in, the smoother your dough will become. Add a little water if needed. If you are not adding colour, then add just enough water to make a smooth, but not sticky, dough.

3 The dough is now ready to roll, model, cut and shape.

4 To bake, place your salt dough shapes on a baking tray lined with grease-proof paper in the oven at the lowest heat. Space them well as the dough may spread. Leave for 1–2 hours, turning your creations occasionally. *An adult should supervise this bit.* When the shapes are hard, turn the oven off but leave them inside to cool completely. Salt dough can also be air-dried, but it will take 1–3 weeks to fully harden.

5 When cool, you can further decorate your creations with paint or pens.

Salt dough beads

These crafty beads are so easy to make. Experiment with lots of different colours and sizes. Larger beads are easier to make as well as being less fiddly to thread. Make them about 1–2 cm in diameter and use a chopstick to make the hole. For smaller beads use a toothpick or wooden skewer to make the holes.

You will need:
Coloured or plain salt dough
Paints and paintbrushes
Chopstick, skewer or toothpick
String for threading

1 Roll a piece of salt dough into a small ball. Using a chopstick or toothpick (depending on the size of your ball), make a hole all the way through the centre of your bead. This may mean your bead ends up a little flatter and not perfectly round, but this is fine.

2 Once you have made as many as you need, place them on a baking tray lined with greaseproof paper and bake in the oven at the lowest heat. Space them out evenly as salt dough has a tendency to spread a bit, the way cookies do.

3 Remove from the oven after 5–8 minutes and reinsert your chopstick or toothpick into the centre of each bead in order to make sure that the hole doesn't close up. Turn the beads over, and return to the oven. Repeat after a further 5–8 minutes and then return to the oven for another hour. Remove the beads from the oven and leave to cool on the baking tray overnight.
An adult should help when handling hot items from the oven.

4 Now you can paint the beads. Once the painted beads are dry, thread on to your string to make a necklace or bracelet. Or both!

Salt dough charms

Make colourful charms for yourself or your friends. This is a great craft to do at a birthday party or during the long school holidays. The hardest part is deciding what to make! You can create any sort of shape, from flowers, hearts and stars to your favourite animals. Use small cookie cutters or mould your own shapes. Flowers are very easy – there are three ways of making them.

You will need:
Coloured salt dough in several
  colours (see page 84)
Toothpick
Small googly eyes
Ribbon, string or leather thong
  for threading
PVA glue

1

2

3

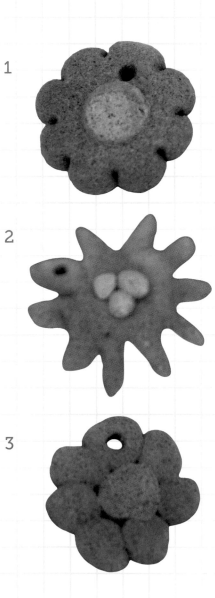

1 To make Flower 1, make a ball, flatten it with your thumb to form a circle, and then use a toothpick to create indentations around the sides for a petal effect. Make a smaller ball in a different colour and press on to the centre. Use the toothpick to make a hole in the top for threading.

2 To make Flower 2, roll ten to twelve sausage shapes, each about 1.5 cm long. Arrange these 'petals' in a circle. Roll three small balls for the centre in a different colour and gently press down to mould the flower together. Use your toothpick to make a hole in one of the petals for threading.

3 To make Flower 3, make six to eight little balls. Arrange them in a flower shape and use your thumb to flatten the petals. Make another ball in a different colour, place in the middle and press down. Use your toothpick to make a hole in one of the petals for threading.

4 To make an owl, roll a small ball and flatten it into an oval shape. Take small pieces of salt dough in different colours and make wings, a beak and feet. Use a toothpick to make a hole in the top for threading. The googly eyes will be added after baking.

5 Try making butterflies, sea creatures, starfish, whales or little monsters – monsters are always great as you can make them up as you go along. Take inspiration from the photographs and create your own.

6 Space out your charms on a baking tray lined with greaseproof paper and bake in the oven at the lowest heat for 1–2 hours. Remember to take the charms out after 5–8 minutes to reinsert the toothpick into the holes.

7 Once they are completely cool, glue on any googly eyes and thread with ribbon or string.

Polymer clay flower cards

Polymer clay is a modelling material that comes in bright colourful blocks and is baked in the oven to harden. It isn't the easiest material to model with, as it can be quite stiff at first and needs kneading to soften up, but the results are worth the hard work. It is often used for modelling jewellery or little figures but you can make pretty much anything with it, including these pretty cards. It's a simple design so is a great way to start crafting with polymer clay.

You will need:
Polymer clay in different colours
Card stock
Paper
PVA glue
Baking tray

1 Roll three small pieces of polymer clay into balls, each one a different size and colour. Don't make them too big.

2 Using your thumb, flatten the first ball on a baking tray. Place the second ball on top and flatten that again and then repeat with the third ball. Your first flower may be too big and rather squashed looking but you will soon get a feel for how big to roll the balls. Make two or three more flowers and place on the baking tray. Make stems out of green polymer clay and join to the flower heads.

3 Bake in the oven, following the manufacturer's instructions – this is usually for 30 minutes at 120°C/230°F. Remove from the oven and leave to cool on the tray.

4 Take a rectangle of coloured card and glue your flowers on with PVA glue. Finally stick the card to a greetings card stock and you're done!

Note: If you want to post the card, you may want to put a couple of sheets of bubble wrap into the envelope to protect the flowers.

Paper Crafts

Magazine beads

These colourful beads can be made from pretty much any old magazines or junk mail you have lying around. It is surprising how colourful your beads will look if you use pages with advertisements on them. For monochrome (black and white) beads, just choose pages with lots of text.

You will need:
Magazines
Straw or toothpick (depending on thread size)
String or elastic
Scissors and PVA glue

1 Cut your page into very long thin triangles. The base of your triangle will determine the width of your bead – here the beads are approximately 1.5 to 2 cm wide. The length of your triangle will determine how thick your beads are. We used triangles approximately 20 cm long.

2 Use a straw to get started as it will help you create more uniform-sized beads. If you want a finer bead, you can use a toothpick – but be careful not to stick your paper to it by accident. Wrap the bottom (wide) end of your triangle around the straw. Apply a little glue to the rest of the triangle and then carefully wrap it around the straw. Keep wrapping, making sure the bead is smooth and tight. Add more glue if needed.

3 Gently slide the bead off your straw or toothpick and allow to dry.

4 Keep making beads in lots of different colours until you have enough to make a necklace or bracelet. Thread on to your string or elastic.

Newspaper bunting

Newspaper bunting is the ultimate in shabby chic and how you make it is up to you. You can sew the edges or keep it simple and use a glue stick; use plain scissors or pinking shears; print with colour or keep it plain. Make it as simple or as complicated as you like! Whatever you choose, you'll have inexpensive and cheerful decorations in no time.

You will need:
Card
Pencil
Scissors
Newspaper
Pinking shears (optional)
Ribbon or string for hanging
Sewing machine (optional)
Glue stick
Paints and stamps (optional)

1 First create a triangular bunting template. Draw a 15 cm line on to a piece of card. Draw a second 15 cm vertical line from the centre (7.5 cm), then join up the points to make a triangle (see diagram on p158). Cut this out for your template.

2 Take a sheet of newspaper and fold it in half. Place the base of your bunting triangle template along the crease. Draw round the template with a pencil and then cut it out, using plain scissors or pinking shears. When you open it up, you will have a diamond shape. Decide how long you want your bunting to be, and cut out as many flags as you need.

3 Fold the diamond shape over your ribbon or string. Then either sew the edge in place with a sewing machine or glue the diamond down. *With younger children, an adult should help with the sewing machine and sew a couple of test strips. Sewing newspaper isn't difficult, but it is fragile and can tear.*

4 Decorate with prints if desired. For example, use corks dipped in paint to create dots or use potato prints to create other shapes and designs.

Newspaper hats

Who loves to dress up? If you do, you may find that your outfit just isn't complete without a fabulous hat. And what better than these gorgeous ones made out of newspaper? They are fun to make and even more fun to wear! They are also perfect for Easter Bonnet parades – it is all down to the details – add chicks and eggs for Easter or flowers for spring decorations.

You will need:
Newspapers
Paints and paintbrushes
Masking tape
Tissue paper
Beads
Tissue and egg chicks (see page 115)
Scissors
PVA glue or glue stick

1. Paint two sheets of newspaper in your chosen colour. Once dry, place the two sheets on top of each other, unpainted sides together, and cut out a large circle.

2. Place the circles on top of the wearer's head, fold down around the head and tape round with masking tape to create a hatband – this will give you a perfect fit! Fold up the sides to create the brim of the hat. You may want to practise with some plain newspaper first as a test run. The basic hat is now finished. Time to decorate!

3. To make flowers for your hat, take four sheets of tissue paper cut into ovals, about 6 cm wide. Stick all the petal pieces together with a little PVA glue or a glue stick, overlapping the ovals so they look like petals. When they have dried, scrunch the petals up a little and glue on a bead or a ball of contrasting tissue paper in the centre. Glue the flowers on to your hat.

4. To make mini eggs, scrunch up pieces of newspaper into a small egg shape. Apply glue to a piece of tissue paper and wrap it around the newspaper. Add a second layer of tissue paper if necessary. Allow to dry and then glue on to the hat.

5. To make little chicks for your hat, follow the instructions for the Tissue paper and egg chicks on page 115. Make a little dent in the hat and glue on green tissue paper leaves to make a nest. Glue the chicks on to your hat.

Wild things

Your favourite books can be a great source of crafty inspiration. Which books do you love? Which characters do you like best? We love *Where the Wild Things Are* by Maurice Sendak. Here are two characters from the book – the Wild Thing and Max. The Wild Thing has big yellow eyes, a big nose, white pointy teeth and a shaggy mane, while Max has a white headpiece with an oval face, a crown, white furry bits and whiskers.

You will need:
Large paper shopping bags
Masking tape
White paper
Paints, including gold acrylic paint,
*   and paintbrushes (if acrylics*
*   are not your thing, use coloured*
*   card or felt)*
White felt or cotton wool
Scissors
PVA glue

1 To make the Wild Thing, shape some horns out of the top of a paper bag, by pressing the bag down slightly in the middle at the top, and securing it with tape.

2 Work out where you need the eyes to go in order to fit the wearer's face and cut out some eye holes.

3 Now you can start painting and decorating. Paint round the eye holes in yellow and add a big red nose. Cut triangles from white paper for the teeth and glue them on. Paint some extra paper dark brown for the shaggy hair and beard. When it is dry, cut it into strips and glue them on to your paper bag mask.

4 To make Max, trim off the bottom part of a paper bag to create a better fit and set aside (you will use this to make the crown).

5 Fit the bag over the wearer's head and mark out where the face should be. Take it off again and cut out the face, remembering to make it an oval shape with a straight edge across the top.

6 Paint the paper bag white. Pinch and glue the sides down a little to make the right shape for Max – the head should be more triangular in shape.

7 Take the piece of trimmed paper from earlier and cut zigzags around the top to make a crown. Paint the crown gold with acrylic paint and tape it to the top of the bag. Glue a strip of white felt or cotton wool around the bottom edge of the crown.

Now you are ready to put your masks on and GO WILD!

Edible
Crafts

Rainbow popcorn

There is nothing quite like sitting down to a movie night at home with some freshly made popcorn. Better still, have a pyjama party and make some rainbow popcorn. This could easily be adapted to make ghoulish black and green popcorn for a Halloween party or pink popcorn for Valentine's... the possibilities are endless! Popping your own corn is much cheaper than buying ready-made and great fun to do.

You will need:
175 g popping corn
2–3 tablespoons sunflower oil
175 g sugar
2 tablespoons water
½–1 teaspoon each of three to four
  colours of liquid food colouring
You will also need one large and one
  small bowl for each colour

1 Start by popping the corn. Take a large pan with a lid and add the sunflower oil. Cover the bottom of the pan with the uncooked popping corn and replace the lid.

2 Place the pan on the hob at full heat. Give the pan a little shake every so often to avoid the popcorn sticking to the bottom. *An adult should supervise this bit.*

3 Listen out for the pop, pop, popping! Keep shake, shake, shaking! Once the popping has stopped, remove from the heat and carefully remove the lid. *Keep children's faces away from the pan as the lid is removed – some corn may still pop out and it will be very hot.* Divide the freshly popped corn into three or four large bowls depending on how many colours you want to use.

4 Place the sugar and water in another pan and bring to the boil. *Again, a grown-up should supervise carefully to avoid an accident.* Keep boiling and stirring until the sugar has all dissolved. Divide the sugary water between three or four small bowls and add food colouring to each.

5 Pour each colour over a bowl of popcorn and keep stirring, tossing and mixing until the popcorn is evenly coloured – you should have nice blue, red, green and yellow popcorn! Combine all the colours together to make your rainbow popcorn.

Notes: Don't make the water and sugar solution too watery, as the popcorn will end up soggy and lose its crispness. If this happens, you can 'save' the popcorn by putting it on a baking tray and placing it in a very low oven for 5–10 minutes.

Some food colouring can have an aftertaste so don't use too much – or try different brands. Sometimes the food colouring may react with the sugar water and you may not get the expected colour (For example, red can turn orange).

Traffic light cookie pops

Take a simple cookie recipe
and have some fun with it.
These traffic light cookie pops
are easy to make and, above all,
yummy to eat – who can resist
chocolate and Smarties? If you
fancy making some cars too,
either buy a car-shaped cookie
cutter or, even better, make
your own!

For the car cookie cutter:

You will need:
Disposable aluminium container
* (takeaway containers are ideal)*
Scissors
Sticky tape

1 Cut a long strip from your foil tray
approximately 2–3 cm wide and
30 cm long. You may have to tape
two pieces together.

2 Shape into a car. You may find it easier
to cut a simple car shape out of card
and bend the foil around this. Make
sure you crease each bend well.

3 Secure in place with a little tape and
the cookie cutter is ready to use.
Don't worry if your shape isn't perfect
as most cookies spread a little in the
oven and so even out any bumps. It
will be a little more fragile than an
ordinary cutter, but works just as well.
Wash gently after use and use again
– but you are likely to only get two to
three batches of cookies out of it.

For the cookies:

You will need:
300 g plain flour
200 g butter, at room temperature
100 g sugar
Baking tray, lined with greaseproof
* paper*
Cooling rack

For the traffic lights:
Lollipop sticks
100 g chocolate
Smarties

For the cars:
Red food colouring
200 g icing sugar
Chocolate buttons

1 Preheat the oven to 180°C/350°F.

2 Place the butter and sugar in a large bowl and cream together well. Make sure your butter is at room temperature before you start as this will make it easier to mix. Add the flour and stir until the mixture is well combined – you may need to get your hands in to press the dough together to bind.

3 Take one half of the dough and, using a rolling pin, roll out to a thickness of about 0.5–1 cm. Use a knife to cut the dough into rectangles about 6 x 3 cm. Carefully push a lollipop stick into the bottom of each rectangle – if you find they poke out a little just cover them up with dough. Place the cookies on a lined baking tray.

4 Knead the remaining dough together, roll out as before and use your cookie cutter to cut out car shapes. Place on the lined baking tray and bake for about 12–15 minutes, checking them from time to time – they should be nice and golden when done. Let them cool slightly before transferring to a cooling rack.

5 Once the cookies are cool, it's time to decorate! Place the chocolate in a heatproof bowl over a pan of gently simmering water. *An adult should help with this bit.* Stir until melted and then spread over the cookies. Add red, yellow and green Smarties to complete your traffic lights. For the cars, place some icing sugar in a bowl and add a few drops of red food colouring and a few drops of water. Stir until you have the right consistency, adding more food colouring or water if necessary. Use a clean paintbrush to paint the icing on to the cars. Stick on chocolate buttons for wheels, using a blob of icing for 'glue'.

Cookie bunting

Another fun thing to make with cookie dough. Mmm... edible bunting, how special is that? Make the bunting as big as you like and decorate to your heart's content or write letters with food gel pens to spell out 'Happy Birthday'.

Makes approximately thirty to forty cookies

You will need:
Card
Aluminium foil
1 quantity of basic cookie dough
 (see page 108)
Knife
Baking tray lined with greaseproof
 paper
Chopstick
Scissors

For the decorations:
Icing sugar
Lemon juice
Food colouring
Selection of sprinkles
Ready-made writing icing (optional)
Ribbon for hanging

1 Preheat the oven to 180°C/350°F.

2 Make a 5 x 5 cm template to cut a triangle from card, then wrap It In foil (this makes it more hygienic).

3 Take your basic cookie dough (see page 108) and roll out the dough to a thickness of about 1 cm. Cookie bunting needs to be a little thicker than ordinary cookies so that it does not break when you hang it.

4 Place your foil-covered template on top of your dough and cut round it with a knife to make triangles. Knead any remaining dough together, roll out again and cut more triangles.

5 Make a hole in the centre of the wide end of each triangle and place them on a lined baking tray. Bake in the oven for 15–20 minutes until they turn golden brown.

6 Remove from the oven. If any holes have closed during baking, use a chopstick to gently re-open while the cookie is still hot. Leave to cool on the baking tray for a few minutes before carefully transferring them to a cooling rack. (If you move them straight from the oven they may break.)

7 When the triangles are fully cooled, it is time to decorate! Start by mixing icing sugar with a little lemon juice and food colouring, taking care not to make it too runny. Spread over the cookies, avoiding the holes you have made, and add some sprinkles. If desired, use ready-made writing icing to spell out a name or write a message.

8 Once your cookies are all dry and set, thread each triangle on to your ribbon. Tie each one gently at the top (to help the cookie face forward) and hang.

You could use small bunting to decorate a cake or hang across a table. You could also make some large bunting triangles for children to decorate at a party and to add to party bags afterwards.

Blown Eggs

Blown Eggs

Blowing and decorating eggs is a wonderful traditional Easter craft. What's more, you can keep your blown eggs for ever – if you're careful – and bring them out year after year. Egg blowing is a bit tricky at first, but once you get the hang of it, it is great fun.

You will need:
Eggs
Drawing pin
Bowl
Toothpick (optional)

1 Very carefully make a small hole in the shell at either end of your egg with your drawing pin. The bigger the hole in the shell, the easier it will be to blow out the yolk and white so make about five or six pricks with the pin, although for a finer result, try making a slightly smaller hole. A good trick is to poke a toothpick into one of the holes in the egg, and use it to break the yolk while it is still inside. This will make it easier to get the yolk out.

2 Holding the egg in both hands over a bowl, place your mouth over the more pointed end of the egg and blow really hard – the inside of the egg should start coming out the other end. Be patient – it can take a while but it is worth the hard work!

3 When the egg is empty rinse under tepid running water. Place upright on a draining rack to allow the egg to dry completely inside and out.

Tissue and egg chicks

These chicks made of tissue paper and eggs are bright, colourful and cheerful – a wonderful craft to do at Easter.

You will need:
Blown eggs (see opposite)
Coloured tissue paper
Paintbrush
Scraps of funky foam,
  felt or card
Googly eyes
Feathers
Scissors
PVA glue

1 Cut your tissue paper into strips and squares and then brush them with PVA glue. Wrap the tissue paper around each egg. Add about three to four layers of tissue paper to each egg.

2 Cut beaks, combs and wattles out of funky foam, felt or card. Glue these on to the eggs. Finally glue on googly eyes and feathers to complete your little chicks.

Egg rabbit & penguin

When decorating your Easter eggs, you can either stick to the traditional, like this little bunny, or go crazy and create other animals such as our penguin here. Or turn them into little round egg people.

You will need:
Blown eggs (see page 114)
Acrylic paints or food colouring and
  vinegar
Paintbrushes
Googly eyes
Scraps of felt, funky foam or card
Black pen
PVA glue

1 First paint or dye your blown eggs. To dye them, mix together 1 cup of lukewarm water, 1 tablespoon of vinegar and 20 drops of food colouring in a cup or small bowl. Add your egg (you may have to weigh the egg down with a spoon), and soak for 15–20 minutes, moving the egg from time to time to make sure it dyes evenly. Remove the egg and gently pat dry with a tea towel. Alternatively, paint the eggs with acrylic paint.

2 Once your eggs are dry, it's time to decorate. To make a bunny, cut bunny ears and a tummy from felt and use PVA glue to attach them to the egg. To make a penguin, cut flippers, a beak and feet from felt and use PVA glue to attach them to the egg.

Note: Because most shop-bought eggs have brown shells, red and green food colourings are likely to give the best results. Different brands of food colouring will yield different levels of success – for example, yellow is very hard to achieve and often turns out red. Use white eggs or duck eggs, if you can find them.

Egg candles

These egg candles make fabulous Easter gifts or decorations. The best thing about them is that no specialist equipment is needed – just some old candles, crayons and eggs!

You will need:
Candle wicks (or see opposite for
* how to make your own)*
Blown eggs (see page 114)
Ends of old white candles
Crayons
Egg cups
Play dough
Old tin cans, washed and dried

1 Follow the instructions on page 114 for blowing your eggs. Rinse the shell out thoroughly and leave to dry completely.

2 Make the hole at the bottom of the egg (the rounder part) a little bigger – you need to be able to pour the wax into it. Insert the candle wick so that it runs right through the egg and comes out of the other hole by about 2 cm.

3 Seal the hole at the pointed end of the egg with some play dough – this will also hold the wick in place. Put the egg in an egg cup with this pointed end facing down.

4 Remove any old wicks from your candle ends (these can also be fished out after the wax has melted). To heat the wax, place an empty tin can into a pan of boiling water and fill it with the white candle ends. Add a piece of wax crayon (about one third of a crayon) to colour the wax and stick to one colour per can. The candle wax and crayon should start to melt straight away. *An adult should supervise and help when handling hot wax and boiling water.*

5 Once the wax is completely melted, remove the can from the pan with an oven glove. Carefully pour the wax into the opening in the eggshell. Wax contracts as it cools so you need to let it cool a little and then top up with more wax to avoid having a dip in your candle. Repeat this three to four times. You will end up with a small dip at the end but it will not be noticeable once the candle is finished.

6 Leave to cool completely before peeling off the shell – sometimes the shell comes off really easily, other times it is a bit trickier! For a really smooth finish, use a hairdryer on a low heat to even out the surface. To allow the candle to stand up on its own (without an egg cup), gently heat a pan and place the base of the egg candle on the bottom of the pan for a couple of seconds – this will give you a flat surface.

Note: To make your own wick, dip a piece of butcher's cotton twine into some melted wax. Repeat three or four times to build up a layer of wax. For best results first soak the twine in a borax/salt solution (4 tablespoons borax and 2 tablespoons salt mixed into 1½ cups of warm water). Leave overnight and then dip the twine into melted wax, as above. You can find borax online but it must be stored away from small hands.

Nature Crafts

Dandelion crown

Say aah! Aren't flowers in the hair just the prettiest thing? Make this little flower crown from dandelions and any other common wild flowers you can find. Sadly they won't last but what better way is there to spend a sunny summer afternoon? You will find that the first crowns you make are a bit fiddly and may well fall apart, but you will soon get the hang of it... and come up with wonderful creations.

You will need:
Freshly picked dandelions (make sure you leave a long stem)
Contrasting flowers (optional)

1 Start with two flowers and lay them down so that the stems cross at right angles. Lift the stem of the first flower over the top of the second and around its own head.

2 Take the third flower and place it under the first two. Bend the stem over the stems of the first and second flowers and around the head of the third flower.

3 Keep going until the garland is long enough to make a little crown. Join the last flower to the first one by threading the stems into the existing loops.

4 Push contrasting flowers, such as daisies or little sprigs of cow parsley, into the crown to finish.

Pressed flowers

Flower pressing is one of those traditional crafts that people have forgotten about – maybe because it sounds a bit complicated and time-consuming. But it's so easy and you don't even need a flower press – a book or notepad and something heavy will do the job just as well. Experiment with different flowers, see what works well and what doesn't – once you start, you'll be hooked, and just want to do it more and more, trying out different techniques and flowers.

You will need:
Large book
Blotting paper
Flowers

1 Pick your flowers, preferably on a dry, sunny day.

2 Position each flower face down or in profile on top of one sheet of paper. Place the second sheet on top and put inside the pages of your book – use something heavy like a telephone directory.

3 Place something heavy on top, such as more books, and leave for 3–4 weeks.

See opposite for a great idea for using your pressed flowers.

Tips:

• *Press your flowers as soon as possible after picking, to avoid any drooping or wilting.*
• *Your flower must be completely dry, otherwise it may go mouldy.*
• *Dried flowers do fade with time, but by avoiding exposure to direct sunlight you can minimise the fading. You can also preserve them for longer by sealing them with découpage glue.*
• *Experiment, experiment, experiment! Some flowers work much better than you think, others won't work at all. Don't forget leaves and grasses.*

Pressed-flower jars

You will need:
Old jars or glasses
Découpage glue or watered down
  PVA glue
Paintbrush
Pressed flowers

1 Paint the outside of your glass or jar with glue. It will dry clear, but you are going to still see brushstrokes. If you want to avoid these, only apply glue to the exact parts that you want to stick your flowers to.

2 Hold your pressed flowers onto the glued surface, attaching them to the jar. Brush a layer of glue over the top. Some flowers may need additional glue. These make lovely little jars for flowers or tea lights.

Grass heads

This is a fun craft that you can do indoors or out. Experience the magic of nature by planting some grass seeds and watching them grow. Chop your little grass head's hair and watch it grow some more. Maybe even give it a crazy hairstyle, such as a mohican?

You will need:
Old nylon tights or pop socks
Soil or compost
Grass seed
Googly eyes
Scraps of felt
Yoghurt pot or flower pot
PVA glue

1 Cut one leg off the pair of tights, making sure there are no holes in the toes! Put 2 or 3 tablespoons grass seed at the bottom of the leg.

2 Add handfuls of soil or compost on top of the grass seeds until you have a good sized ball. You will need more soil than you think. Tie a knot tightly above it. You will have a ball of earth (the head) and a long piece of tights material hanging down. Keep this as it will help with 'watering' your grass head later.

3 Pinch a bit of the head and twist to make a nose. Secure it by tying with a piece of cotton, string or an elastic band. This can be a little fiddly so just take your time. Use PVA glue to add googly eyes and a felt mouth.

4 Place your grass head in a yoghurt pot or flower pot (with no holes), with the long piece of the tights tucked into the pot. Add water – the tights dangling into the water will soak it up and make sure the head stays moist. If you want to speed up the process, you can give the head a quick shower under the tap to moisten the earth the first time round. Take care not to make it too wet or your grass head will get mouldy and your googly eyes may fall off. Slightly moist is good. Soggy is not. Place in a sunny spot and watch as grass hair sprouts and starts to grow.

5 Add a little water to the pot every 3–4 days. After 10–12 days you should have enough grass to give your grass head its first haircut.

Stick men

There is no craft as simple or as fun as these stick men. The next time you go for a walk, remember to gather a few sticks!

You will need:
Sticks
Googly eyes
Scraps of fabric
PVA glue

1 Take a stick – look for ones with interesting bumps.

2 Add some googly eyes and glue on some fabric scraps. You're done! How easy was that?

128

Lavender wand

Lavender wands look and smell wonderful. They make pretty decorations or can be used to gently fragrance your clothes drawer. You could also add them to a fairy costume to complete that whimsical look! You will need nine to fifteen stalks per wand, depending on the thickness of your lavender.

130

You will need:
Lavender stalks
Long piece of narrow ribbon

1 Pick your lavender – cut as low as you can to the root so that the stems are as long as possible. It should also be quite young, so that you can bend the stalks without breaking them.

2 Trim the stems of any leaves and gather into a bunch – make sure you have an uneven number of stems.

3 With the lavender flowers facing away from you, tie a piece of ribbon around your bunch, just where the flowers meet the stems.

4 Take one of the stems and fold it away from you, over the flowers and the ribbon. Fold down the second stem but this time tuck the ribbon under it. The third stem goes over the ribbon and the fourth stem under. Continue in this way – you are beginning a round of weaving! With an uneven number of stems you will be able to just continue to go round and round, weaving your ribbon in and out of the stems. It gets easier as you go along and the wand starts to take shape.

5 When you get to the bottom, wrap the ribbon around the stems and tie in a knot. If you want you can leave a length of ribbon for hanging in cupboards.

Turtle and crab shell magnets

Collecting shells is a favourite seaside pastime – it is so lovely walking along the beach and seeing what treasures you can find. Then, when you get home, you can make something crafty with them. Shells are from the sea, so why not use them to make some little sea creatures – crabs and turtles, perhaps. Add a little magnet and you have fun fridge magnets to remind you of your holiday or day at the seaside.

You will need:
Large shells
Acrylic paints and paintbrushes
Red pipe cleaners (two for each crab)
PVA glue
Googly eyes
Stiff green card or funky foam
Large magnets

1 Paint your shells red and green and leave to dry. You can also colour them using the method used for the Crayon and rock paperweights (see page 64) – this will give you a nicely textured surface.

2 To make the crab, cut one pipe cleaner into eight pieces for the legs. Cut the second pipe cleaner in half and form some claws at the ends.

3 Tuck the pipe cleaners under the shell (so that the legs are pointing right up in the air) and glue in place. By tucking it in, the pipe cleaner is holding itself in place while it is drying. You can rearrange the legs once the glue has dried. Glue on googly eyes.

4 Cut some card to the same size as the shell and glue to the underside of the shell – this gives you a surface to stick the magnet to.

5 To make the turtle, place your shell on top of the card or funky foam, and draw around the shell. Then draw on a head, 4 flippers and a tail to create the outline of a turtle. All shells are different so you will need to use your imagination and draw your own turtle outline.

6 Cut out your turtle shape, and rub out any pencil marks. Glue the shell on to the turtle shape and add googly eyes.

7 Once dry, glue a strong magnet to the bottom of the sea creatures and attach them to your fridge.

Pine cone owls and babies

Pine cones are a wonderful autumn craft material. They can be turned into so many things! These owls are perfect for Halloween and make lovely seasonal decorations while the pine cone babies would look sweet hanging from a Christmas tree.

Pine cone owl

You will need:
Pine cone
Googly eyes
Scraps of funky foam, felt or card
Feathers
Ribbon for hanging (optional)
Scissors
PVA glue

1 Cut large and small circles from your foam or felt in contrasting colours. These will form the bases for your owl's eyes. You can use coins as templates or do it freehand. Glue your two circles together and add the googly eyes. Use any tiny scraps of felt or foam to make owl eyebrows.

2 Place the pine cone on the table and check that it 'sits' naturally – you want your owl to be able to sit unaided. Once you have done this, add the eyes and beak to the front with lots of glue – you need a lot, as the pine cone doesn't have a smooth surface area to glue your pieces to. The PVA will dry clear, so don't worry if you can see it at this stage.

3 Glue some feathers on to the pine cone to complete your owl and tie a ribbon on if required.

Pine cone babies

You will need:
Scraps of felt in different colours
Scraps of ribbon
Wooden bead, approximately 1.5 cm
  in diameter
Small pine cone
Hot glue gun or wood glue
Paint and paintbrush or black pen

1 Cut a triangle with one long edge from one colour of felt and a flower from another colour – the easiest way to make a flower is to cut a circle, nip it eight times and then round off the nipped parts into petal shapes.

2 Cut a small hole in the triangle, close to the long side, and a small hole in the centre of the flower. Cut a length of ribbon, loop it, then thread it through the triangle, the bead and the flower and tie a knot in the end. (See diagram on p158.)

3 Flatten the pointy bit of your pine cone by pressing it on the table gently. This will help nestle the top half of your baby better.

135

4 Use a hot glue gun or wood glue to glue the triangle on to the bead, the bead on to the flower, and the flower on to the pine cone. Add a bit of extra glue to make the petals point down a little.

5 Paint on the eyes and mouth.

Note: If you are using wood glue, there will be a certain amount of sitting there and holding the bits until they dry. That is what is so amazing about hot glue guns – everything sets so quickly!

Conker pencil toppers

There are two exciting things about autumn, one is that school starts, and the other is that soon gorgeous glossy conkers will start to fall from the trees. Those wonderfully brown and shiny conkers are irresistible. Once you have gathered a few, what will you make with them? Pencil toppers of course! They will shrivel with time (as all conkers do), but they will not lose their charm.

You will need:
Conkers
Knitting needle or skewer
Pencil
Funky foam or felt
Black pen
Googly eyes (optional)
Scissors
Hot glue gun or strong PVA glue

1 Decide on the animals you would like to make and make the most of any irregularities in the conker – for example, a bump could be the nose of a bear.

2 Use a knitting needle or skewer to make a hole in the bottom of the conker and push your pencil into the hole.

3 Cut shapes for ears and other features from funky foam or felt and glue on. For the bear's ears, cut slits into the chestnut with a sharp knife, insert the ears and glue in place. *Care should be taken when using sharp knives – an adult should help and supervise.*

4 Draw the faces using a black pen and add googly eyes, if using.

As the chestnut will shrink with time, you may find that the pencil hole becomes a little loose. If this happens, just add a little Blu-tack to help secure your pencil.

Acorn creatures

Acorns are another fun natural material to craft with in autumn – you will find plenty of them in your local woods. In early autumn, acorns will still be green and soft. Gather a selection and get making!

You will need:
Acorns
Skewer or knitting needle
Long thin twigs
Cotton wool
Black pen
PVA glue

1 To make an acorn animal, check which way around your acorn will look best, and incorporate the natural features into your design, such as a little animal nose or the markings on the animal's chest.

2 Use your skewer to prick four holes at the bottom of one acorn and one on top of it – you might need to give the skewer a good wiggle to make the holes big enough for the twigs. Break a twig into five little sticks and insert them into the holes to make legs and a neck. Prick a hole in another acorn and push on to the neck.

3 To make a horse, add two little twigs for ears. To make a sheep, glue on a little cotton wool fleece. To make a person, add an acorn cup for a hat. Draw on eyes to finish.

Halloween & Christmas Crafts

Halloween satsuma lanterns

Halloween doesn't have to mean 'scary' — cute works just as well. If you don't have the time or the inclination to carve a big pumpkin, then why not try these mini satsuma jack-o'-lanterns?

You will need:
Two or three satsumas or
* mandarins ('easy-peelers' are best)*
Sharp knife
Spoon
Nail scissors
Tea lights

1 Slice off the top of each satsuma using a sharp knife and then scoop out the flesh with a spoon. If you create a little tear, don't worry — you can incorporate it in the final design by cutting some zigzags into the top.

2 Give the peel a good wash and make sure all the flesh has been scooped out.

3 Using a pair of nail scissors, cut a face into the satsuma shell. As satsumas are small and slightly tricky to work with, simple designs are best.

4 Add a tea light and watch your mini Halloween lanterns glow! You will find that the peel will dry and stiffen, maybe even curl in a bit after a few days. This isn't a bad thing, just different!

Jam jar lanterns

These jar lanterns are great for lighting indoors but work just as well outside – the wind won't get to them and trick-or-treaters will know that you are expecting them if you put a few of them outside your front door.

You will need:
Large jam jar
Orange tissue paper
Black paper
Old paintbrush
Black ribbon (optional)
Tea light
Scissors
PVA glue

1 Cut or tear your orange tissue paper into small pieces. Cut jack-o'-lantern face shapes from black paper. Triangles and spiky mouths are classic shapes to use, but you can use your imagination.

2 Dilute PVA glue with water so that it reaches a milky consistency (approximately one part water to two parts glue). Apply liberally to the outside of the jar, using an old paintbrush.

3 Add your tissue papers to the lantern and flatten them down. Then add another layer of glue and more tissue paper – you do not need to let the glue dry between layers. Finish with a layer of diluted glue for a glossy finish.

4 Position the eye and mouth shapes and add a final layer of glue. Leave to dry completely before tying some black ribbon around the rim of the jar (optional). Simply pop in a tea light and you are ready to go!

Note: Never leave candles burning unattended.

Advent calendar

Christmas is all about traditions. Most of our favourite traditions signal the beginning of the festive season. Christmas carols on the radio. The first mince pie. Opening the first door on your Advent calendar. What will be inside? A chocolate coin? A message? A joke? Make your own Advent calendar and every year fill it with special messages, a little poem or small treats.

You will need:
12 pieces of felt in assorted colours,
* each measuring 23 x 23 cm*
Star template
Needle and embroidery thread
Felt numbers (or cut your own)
PVA or fabric glue
Ribbon
Safety pins (optional)

1 Draw a star shape on to a piece of card, cut out to make a template. Cut out twenty-four pairs of stars from your coloured felts. You should get two pairs of stars from each sheet of felt.

2 Take a pair of stars and, using a running stitch (see p159), sew around your star through both thicknesses, but only through one thickness at the top point, leaving an opening so you can add your Advent surprises.

3 Glue on the felt numbers.

4 String all the stars on to a long length of fine ribbon.

Time to fill with surprises!

Orange slices

Dried orange slices are a very quick and satisfying craft for Christmas. They have a lovely rustic look but are really cheerful and Christmassy. Once dried, simply hang them on a ribbon and your decoration is done!

You will need:
Oranges
Knife
Oven rack
Oven gloves
Ribbon

1 Preheat your oven to low – approximately 120°C/230°F. Cut your oranges horizontally into slices approximately 1 cm wide so that each slice has a nice segmented pattern.

2 Place your orange slices on a rack in the oven (if you put them on a baking tray they will stick) and bake for approximately 2–3 hours, turning two or three times. Check them regularly, especially during the first 30 minutes when they are most likely to stick. *An adult should supervise when using a hot oven.*

3 At this point they will still have retained a little moisture, but they are ready for crafting or hanging and will dry out completely during the Christmas period. They will last indefinitely if stored in a dry environment. Simply thread a fine ribbon through one edge and knot to form a loop for hanging.

Paper baubles

The run-up to Christmas is a great time of year to sit down together and get crafty. Why not make one new Christmas decoration for the Christmas tree every year? These little paper baubles can be made from your child's paintings or old Christmas cards, can include family photos or can be shaped into Christmas trees. Try making them egg-shaped for a sweet Easter tree decoration.

You will need:
Thick paper or thin card
Pencil
Ribbon or cord for hanging
Scissors
Glue stick

1 Use a glass or similar round object to mark out eight to ten circles on your chosen paper or card. If you are adding photographs, find and cut out pictures that are approximately 2 cm smaller in diameter. For an egg or tree decoration, cut out eight to ten identical shapes from your card.

2 Cut your circles, eggs or tree shapes out as neatly as possible. If you are adding photographs, glue them on to the circles.

3 Fold each circle in half and make a good crease. If you are using tree or egg shapes, fold them in half vertically.

4 Glue the left side of one crease of the circle or card shape to the right side of another. Continue until you have glued all but two of your pieces together.

5 Attach a loop or ribbon or cord for hanging then glue the back of the first half circle to the last half circle to create a sphere. Even them all out a bit if necessary and add a tiny bit more glue to the top of the bauble to secure the ribbon.

Angel Christmas tree toppers

The top of a Christmas tree is a very special place so you will need a very special angel to sit there. We looked to the Orthodox Church for inspiration to create these toilet roll angels in rich colours – reds, greens and, of course, lots of gold. If you are worried about your painting skills, remember that you are only using toilet rolls and that there are plenty more where your first one came from. If you make a mistake, just paint over it or start again. Having said that, it is a good idea to do a little sketch of your angel first.

You will need:
Toilet roll tube
Pencil
Card
Paints (red, green, brown, pink, yellow, white and gold)
Paintbrushes
Black pen
Scissors
PVA glue

1 Do a rough sketch of your angel so that it is clear in your head where the face, wings and any other details are to go. Copy the sketch loosely on to your toilet roll tube.

2 Begin by painting on the face and hands, then the hair and finally the body, making sure each colour is dry before you add a new one over the top. Leave to dry and then add any details in gold.

3 Cut out your wings and a circle for the halo from a piece of card and paint in your desired colours.

4 Add any details to the wings and face with a black pen – it's best to keep it as simple as possible.

5 Glue the wings and halo on to the tube. If necessary, hold in place with a clothes peg while the glue dries and sets.

Christmas stocking

Convert an old favourite jumper into a jolly Christmas stocking! You will get the knitted look without the hard work of knitting. If you are lucky you may get two stockings out of one jumper – it all depends on the size of the sweater.

You will need:
Newspaper or card
Old jumper
Needle and thread
Sewing machine
Ribbon (optional)
Scraps of felt
Buttons and embroidery thread
 for decorating
Scissors

1 Make a template by drawing a stocking shape on a piece of newspaper or a large piece of card and cut out.

2 Cut the jumper at the seams. Take the two largest pieces, put them right sides together and pin the template in place.

3 Either machine or hand stitch around the template and then cut out your stocking leaving a 1–2 cm seam allowance. Turn right sides out.

4 Create a loop out of ribbon for hanging the stocking. Alternatively use the cuffs or offcuts from the sweater to form a loop. Stitch in place.

5 Cut out your child's initial from felt and stitch on to the stocking using a running stitch (see p159). Stitch on little felt shapes, such as snowflakes, Christmas trees or holly leaves, and buttons to finish.

Ice ornaments

After the excitement and sparkle of Christmas, January and February can feel a little dark and cold. This is when these ice ornaments can bring a bit of natural cheer to your garden or window. Certainly one reason to look forward to the freezing weather!

You will need:
Shallow plastic dishes, such as picnic plates and bowls
Tray
String
Selection of found objects (holly berries and leaves, shells, sticks, small stones)

1 Arrange your dishes on a tray, to make carrying them outside easier. Fill the dishes with water.

2 Take a piece of string that is about 20 cm long and dip one end in the water. Make sure it is properly submerged so that it freezes securely into your ornament.

3 Place your berries, leaves and twigs in the water. When you take your dishes outside, they will move around, so don't worry too much about arranging them in a specific way.

4 Carry the tray outside and leave to freeze overnight. Ease the ornaments out of their dishes – if they are stuck, run briefly under a hot tap to loosen.

5 Hang outside on the branches of a tree or from windows.

Note: You can make these in your freezer too, whatever the weather, but they won't last very long when it's not below zero outside!

Diagrams

Sausage dog and giraffe marionettes p28–33

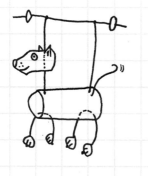

Clothes peg people p36

For the mermaid's hair:

Monkey p40

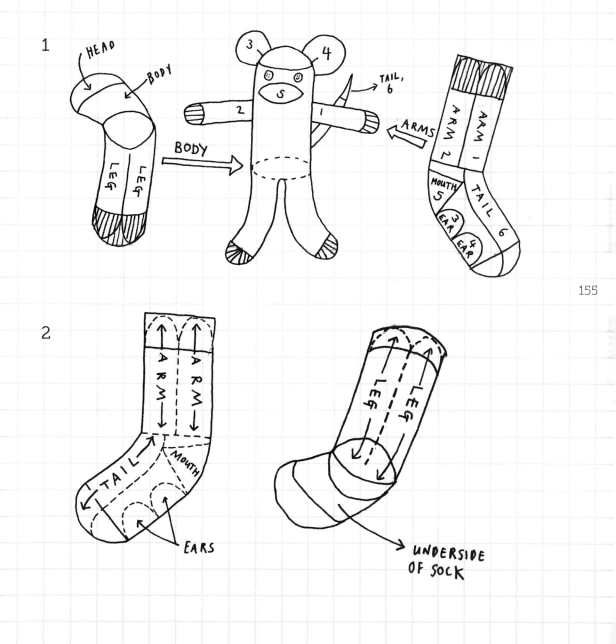

1

HEAD
BODY

3
4
TAIL, 6
2
S
1

BODY

ARMS

ARM 1
ARM 2
MOUTH 5
3 EAR
4 EAR
TAIL 6

LEG
LEG

2

ARM
ARM
TAIL
MOUTH

EARS

LEG
LEG

UNDERSIDE
OF SOCK

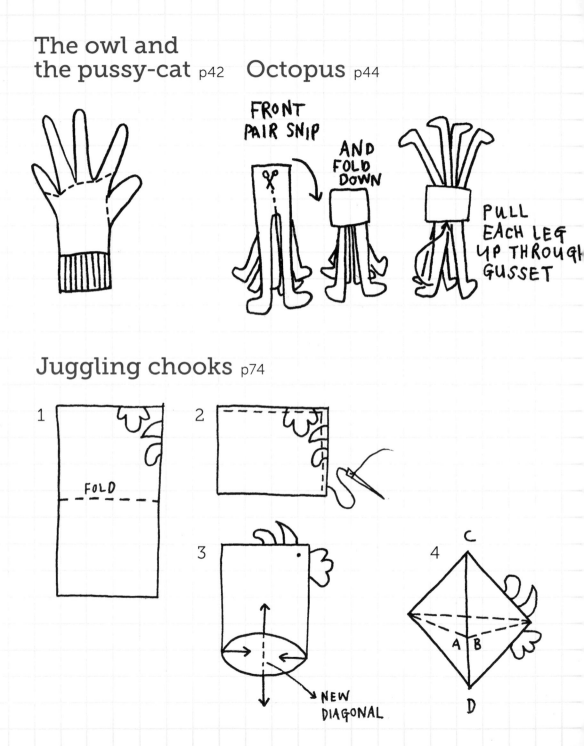

The owl and
the pussy-cat p42

Octopus p44

FRONT
PAIR SNIP

AND
FOLD
DOWN

PULL
EACH LEG
UP THROUGH
GUSSET

156

Juggling chooks p74

1

FOLD

2

3

NEW
DIAGONAL

4

C

A B

D

iPod case p76

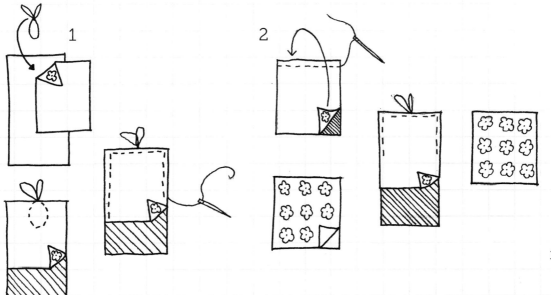

1

2

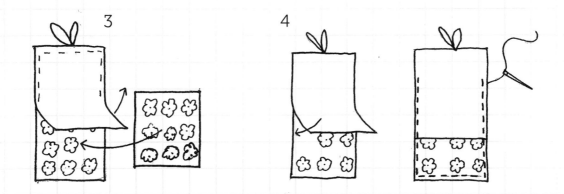

3

4

Felt doughnut p78

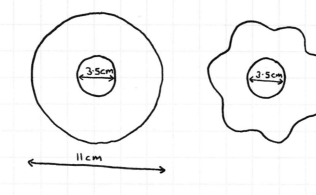

DOUGHNUT TEMPLATE   ICING TEMPLATE

Newspaper bunting
p96

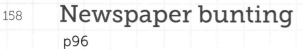

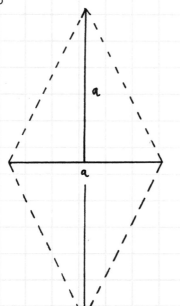

Pine cone babies
p134

Simple stitches

Running stitch

Blanket stitch

Chain stitch

French knot

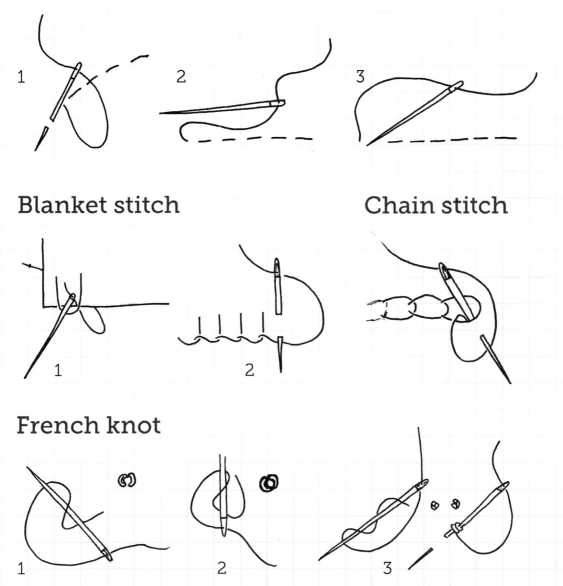

Acknowledgements

Thank you to my wonderfully supportive an enthusiastic husband, James and mother-in-law, Margaret. Without your help and encouragement Red Ted Art would not be where it is now.

Thank you to my good friends Ali and Maren, for loving everything I do and believing in me from the word go.

Thank you to Andrea, Chelsea, Nina, Ali and Kelly for going through the WHOLE book with me and giving invaluable feedback on how to make it better.

Thank you to Sarah from www.maisoncupcake.com for sharing her cookie bunting idea; to Liz from www.http://missielizzie-meandmyshadow.blogspot.co.uk/ for sharing the organza flowers; and to Aly from http://plus2point4.co.uk/ for her felt strawberry craft!

And finally to all you wonderful readers of www.redtedart.com, without your readership, comments and support, I may never have continued with the website and never written this book!